MOTHERLANDS

Motherlands

VAREESHA KHAN

RESOURCE *Publications* • Eugene, Oregon

MOTHERLANDS

Copyright © 2024 Vareesha Khan. All rights reserved. Except for brief quotations in critical publications or reviews, no part of this book may be reproduced in any manner without prior written permission from the publisher. Write: Permissions, Wipf and Stock Publishers, 199 W. 8th Ave., Suite 3, Eugene, OR 97401.

Resource Publications
An Imprint of Wipf and Stock Publishers
199 W. 8th Ave., Suite 3
Eugene, OR 97401

www.wipfandstock.com

PAPERBACK ISBN: 979-8-3852-2196-7
HARDCOVER ISBN: 979-8-3852-2197-4
EBOOK ISBN: 979-8-3852-2198-1

08/28/24

Contents

Acknowledgments | vii

Native (i.) | 1

city of ghosts | 5

Harem | 8

Relative | 9

veer zara | 11

colonies | 12

Bacchanalia Ballads | 14

plea | 15

Split | 17

Divided (i.) | 18

Divided (ii.) | 20

2k | 22

asterisk | 24

KHI | 26

parro pappo | 27

background | 28

an ancient memory | 30

1254 | 31

Who's going to take care of nana? | 33

Photographing Karachi | 35

basharam | 37

To all the women who had sacrificed | 39

what it means to be a woman | 43

What your mother tells you | 44

Legacy | 46

Native (ii.) | 48

About the Author | 51

Acknowledgments

I would like to express my deepest gratitude to my partner Najeeb for his unwavering support throughout this journey.

Native (i.)

My tongue stutters, stumbling to pronounce my own name,
The whispers of its syllables, soft and breathless,
Overtaken, by sharp winds, brought by winters,
Now almost two decades in the making.

My ancestors never felt this cold,
They wandered, instead, in the oasis of Asia,
With sweet *aam*, spicy *tikka*, and crispy *makkai*,
At lunch, I am given the choice between a hamburger or pizza,
I go with pizza.
Cheese only, please.

So, we take pride in our new abodes,
But moving boxes that are never quite unpacked,
Rip out tendrils that just began to take root,
Fertilized soil with seeds plucked out,
Eventually, you learn not to bother planting at all.

Asia giving earthquakes of culture shock,
Magnitude 6 coming your way,
When you step out of the airport,
And see people who look like you,
More than people who don't look like you at all,
And you breathe in the aroma of a country you began to forget,
And you wonder what life would have been like if you never left.

The sands of distance, however,
Erode with time, the link between home and birthplace,
Your history becomes a foreign land,
Drawing blanks as you try to translate,
The English that has spread into your veins,
Neither West nor East nor North nor South,

Tugging on your mother's scarf to whisper what color *churiyan* you want,
Into her ear, too hesitant, too frightened to speak out loud,
The exposure of your voice, with the accent of she left saying quite plainly,
I'm not from here anymore.

Sunday mornings you are woken up by the sounds of your parents,
Shouting into the phone *hello hello can you hear me?* in Urdu,
Desperate to sew oceans back together,
From calling cards found in ethnic enclaves to the green WhatsApp icon,
Pulling relatives close to close the distance,
I stay silent when they call me over,
I return to my room, and pull out my French assignment.
Je m'oublie.

History is discarded, replacing memories with legacy,
Turning ancestors into refugees,
Immigrants, under the weight of two worlds,
And without roots to latch onto,
Drown easily when flooded with change,
Assimilation shows up as a lifeguard,
But shakes the integrity of your spirit,
When it costs the sum of all you ever were.

I've become claustrophobic with conflicting identities,
Pressing against my skin,
The questions brought by past and present,
Cutting at my throat, and frustrating my future,
Pushing me further from the shore,
Adrift, drowning seems imminent,
So, you begin to look for anchors,
Just to sink.

The certainty of faith draws a believer a warm bath during frigid hardships,
But the task of believing crashed waves higher than tsunamis,
Pulling me under over and over,
I never learned how to swim,
Like the whispers that have left my name,
So had the possibility of peace.
The crisis of faith made robust by the paths of nomads,
Like friends and school, God comes and goes,
Ebbs and flows, without anything permanent to hold onto,
Sometimes you pray to God just to feel something,
Sometimes you pray to God just to feel nothing.
Sometimes you don't pray at all.

But identity doesn't leave you,
Your skin is marked, your passport is marked,
Reminded by the checkboxes of forms and the rhetoric of the news,
Belonging impossible, but escaping more impossible still.
Eventually, you hit the ocean floor, yet water has not flooded your lungs.
Somehow, I'm still breathing.

So, you learn the paths of currents,
And the texture of coral,
Underwater, the voices from above are muddled,
And your soul begins to echo from shells,
Building buoyancy into your flesh,
Rising to the surface on your own island,
Is this what it feels like to be a native?

Boundaries of countries stratify with pigmentation,
But leave out homes for those lost in the spaces between continents,
So, we must hunt for something to believe in,
When the desire to belong roars in our ears,

Easing the aches of our souls with the promise to find paradise,
And if all else fails, make within ourselves a sanctuary.

city of ghosts

A presence I cannot name,
Anaphors to my antecedents,
Orbiting out in space,
Unable to touch,
Petal shards that fall,
And settle into cement,
I keep returning to cities of the dead,
In the hopes of naming the ghosts,

Unnerving to come as a visitor,
When eventually, we all must host,

The guests who come and want to know,
Because there is no one to ask,
Not really, only given clues,
Even the living can't recollect,

We become detectives, investigating our history,
I want to know all the things my mother told me,
And trace it back, to my forefather's stories,

My nana will tell me her nana's quirks,
And laugh in remembrance,

Time airbrushes history,
And I am looking for the roots of the trauma,
In her old age, she rather forget,

I need to know what runs in the family,
This family that keeps running,
From shahjahanpur to dacca to sekar to karachi,
To riyadh, to ames, to troy, to ann arbor, to montreal,
To windsor, to toronto, to calgary, to buffalo, to chicago,

I have a mole on the bottom of both of my feet,
My mother, worried, tells me that a mole on the foot, is the sign of the traveler, the nomad,
She threatens to cut both of mine out,

I've been all around the world?
What am I looking for?

Going back home, I begin the search,
Through troves of documents, just to catch a glimpse,
Of what my dada was like, what made him who he is?
In a black-and-white west pakistani ID card,
I dissect his face, his expression, the way his eyes look off far into the distance,

Am I learning anything? Or just projecting my own life onto his?

They say within three generations, you will be forgotten,
But I need to know because what isn't known can easily be passed down,
Until it becomes tradition and ritual,
Until it codes itself into DNA,

I'm plagued by the inarticulation,
Of relatives that never put to words, their thoughts unwritten,
Petals that fall, fragments of who we are,
I return to the cemetery,
With a macabre urge to pull out a Ouija board and get down to the truth,

If it exists even, I do not know,
And who would even tell me if it does?
We're always reinventing, a narrative that's never static,

At the heart of it all,
To know myself, I'm trying to know who my mother and father are,
If I knew the roots of their neuroses,
For every failure of parenting, I could forgive them and blame someone else,
And repeat the cycle until I have forgiven everyone,
But what's done is done,
The city of dead won't welcome any guests,

My prologue is blurry,
I will have to invent —
Grasp at straws and pretend,
Let the petals fall where they may,
And plant new roses instead.

Harem

Walking into a Moroccan hammam, I am thrown by the femininity,
A chorus of women soaking nude in steamed baths,
Perfume permeates.
I ache for belonging in this unfamiliar space,
For the close confidantes of sisters,

Back home, I feel the same pangs,
An outsider to this womanhood, I can only watch and try to learn this foreign tongue,
An unbreakable unit singing in sync at wedding *dholkis*,
The expertise of henna painted on by your aunts and cousins,

Even in the house it bustles,
Coordination that rivals the military as dishes are made and clothes are cleaned,
A harem in the truest sense,
A secret world denied to men,
I feel like a man peering in,
Unable to join the rhythm,
Never used to this kind of girlhood,

Life abroad denies you such tangible solidarity,
No one to teach you these skills that back home are so innate,
Off-beat and off-pitch, it's clear I lack the rituals,

At the hammam, I stick to the walls,
I look at the baths,
I don't jump in.

Relative

North American winters lay bare the loneliness,
Another season of snow, surrounded by no one you know,
Another move, another new city,
Another space you can never call your own,

While your relatives don't bother to knock, just enter,
Each other's homes, just down the street,
Babes swaying back and forth in their mothers' arms,
Smiles on my cousins' faces, as they know when they're older, there will always be a gaggle of kids to call outside for a cricket game,
The family that left barely leave a trace,

We struggle and try to rebuild the magic here,
We persuade others to make the change,
But by then it's already too late,

A childhood lived alone leaves such a hole,
It takes a generation to fill,

The house feels empty without the laughter,
When there's no one with to share,
No memories take place,
When you move again, it's just checking out of a hotel,
Gone without a fuss or anyone to beg you to stay,

Relatives begin to become relative,
As friends and relations cobble into a new kind of family,
But nothing soothes the soul quite the same,
As your kin all lounging on the couch or sneaking off for a late-night adventure,

Every time we come back, we try to stuff in as much as we can into a two-week vacation,
I barely know you,
But how come it feels so easy to erase the years of distance?
It's bittersweet at the airport,
Family to strangers to family again,

I return to Chicago,
I am itching to buy another plane ticket.

veer zara

India — an estranged cousin,
Yet still the home of all my grandparents,
It never quite made sense,

When my mother would tell me to stay away,
I come closer,
Like a moth drawn to a taboo flame,

Even in my youth I treated India more like a half-sibling,
Intriguing in its difference,

My mom told me to avoid Indians,
And here I am, marrying one,

Maybe it stems from the displacement,
Being kicked out from your home,
My mother calls her uncle, who never left,
As she wishes warm greetings for his daughter's wedding,
That she isn't allowed to attend,

My Indian friends live in the reverse,
Their grandmothers warning to not make friends with Pakistanis,
While grabbing chai with their Lahori neighbors,

Living under the growing rhetoric that replaces diversity with nationalist fervor,
There must be space for a different kind of way,

Let's meet in Kashmir,
The adopted child everyone has staked a claim to,
In the most remote mountain,
Away from the conflict,
A *veer-zara* kind of story,
What would it have been like if we never broke up?

colonies

The last of the beautiful things,
The final frontier before decay sets in,
A colonial history that just won't rub off,
Even when wrung and twisted, nothing splits,
And the indigo dye stains the homeland with English,

The cream and red fort of the Empress Market remains unfazed by the city's deconstruction,
We welcome the colonizers and their fair complexion, slapped into a pedestal of the highest ideal of beauty,
Even willing to push our own sun-kissed kin lower to feel closer to whiteness,
We traverse over the bloody bodies of everyone thrown overboard when the colonial project became inconvenient,
Altering our intonations to come off assimilated,

At *Le Coloniale*, I am awed at the blatant honesty,
Vietnamese food at French prices,
Black-and-white photographs depicting colonial horrors in full display,
I wonder why it's so overt; it's hard to look away,
I keep coming back,

In London, I step out with a strangeness,
It's a funny experience visiting your colonizer's country,
A small chunk of land packed with descendants of a marred history,
I'd fly back right now if I could,
The Indian food is to die for,

Landing in Karachi, I am not sure which side of the coin I bring,
My skin brown and my voice white,
Trading in a currency cache to spend decadently,

A blue passport backing up the implicit power and threat the diaspora brings,

It's a twisted thing, so full of contradictions,
Heralding the military and denouncing military occupation,
Loving the colonizer and hating it just the same,

I mix broken Urdu into my perfect English,
I am weaving in the dissonance.

Bacchanalia Ballads

When god is music, why is it such a sin to sing?
When god is energy, why is it such a sin to dance?
Why do we break the harmony into stillness?

When the divine lifted my soul, all I heard was music,
A cascading of harps, wrapped gold ribbons of melody,
Heaven is an orchestra,
So why are we falling silent?
The energy, the movement, the meaning of being alive,
Static, I am suffocating,
Might as well be a rock stuck in ritual,
Why can't I break out into ecstasy?

Where is our Bacchanalia, our rapture?
When the arrow of love hits, can't that scream ring out like the opera, pain transformed into beauty?

I feel more akin to my Sufi ancestry,
Carving out a space for intense living,
Etching love and all it entails into a voice that sails,
Above the rest, above the rest, we find the chorus,
That connects,
We find the beat, the beat that breaks,
Away all the illusions and echoes a new way to stay,

Light my soul and I will break out or break off,
Untethered, a voice lost at sea.

plea

can you forgive me for not knowing?
not knowing with fluency,
the strum of the *strithar*,
how was i supposed to know?
when all around me,
they sang the praises instead of the guitar.

can you forgive me for taking too long to
feel the pop of coriander seeds,
for not knowing the crunch,
the burst of surprise,
i've been snacking on popcorn mindlessly.

when everyone asked for a pizza party,
can you forgive me for not advocating,
for the celebrations of samosas,
that we share together on *eid*?

when so much of our poetry lavishes our spices,
here i am drawing a blank,
when i open up my mother's pantry,
and can't pick out the right brown powder,
to make the right recipe,
in the right way?
can you forgive me for using a *shaan* packet instead?

can you forgive me for being so meek,
never willing to drape myself with all the *raang*,
denying myself every shade of indigo,
if only because,
i would be the only one.

a culture that's not quite my own,
with time it feels like appropriation,
can you forgive me,
for not knowing the feeling of home?

Split

Unknot with me this tension,
Of culture and religion,

All these rules, most people can't trace back to a verse or a saying,

Imparted by a quilt of characters,
Always a claim to the divine truth, whatever that is,
The logic that never can bear the weight of living,

Told to cover up,
By the ones who are meant to not mind,
Told to be modest,
By the ones who are meant to look away,

All these contradictions, a tightrope that becomes a tripwire,
Traps everywhere, you'd have to shrink yourself smaller than a mouse to escape,

If this Gordian Knot won't untie,
My hands will have to become knives,
To cut through all the bullshit,
A breakthrough that looks like running away.

Divided (i.)

I am trying to trace these stories,
In their voices I don't detect the root,
As they recant the recollections with a clinical detachment,
But how can we ignore the displacement of the displaced?
When trauma floods, it is our generation that feels the splatter,
A bucket that overflows, onto us, how can we ignore?

I try to imagine my dad's father, zipping in and out of his hotel lobbies now suddenly packing his bags,
His life in India stamped out as he realizes it's not safe anymore to stay,

Somehow in Dhaka he flourishes,
With several kids now in tow,
Running an import export business, a business almost like himself,

My dad grows up in this life of luxury,
That slowly gets taken away,
As the seventies roar in with unrest, and another civil war exports them out,

Now in Karachi their world uncertain,
Not able to thrive in the same way,
Soon it all begins to decay,
Money that used to pop out of the ether, now is picked sparse from pillowcases,
What was supposed to be a quick trot over to see relatives now becomes a permanent visitation,
Somehow in all this, my grandparents stayed generous,
Never knowing a no, always dolling out for neighbors and the homeless,

Only my oldest uncle and aunt remember the good times, my dad was born too late to know,
I try to poke and pry for more answers, of how all this disruption played out,
In the quiet that leaves much to desire,
I have to fill in the blanks myself.

Divided (ii.)

My mother's sister tells me of her visit a decade ago to her uncle in Uttar Pradesh,
How it feels to go back to a life would have had if you had never left,
As I jostle around in a rickshaw, I wonder the same,
About a life here versus what I've known for so long,
It seems we all imagine what could have been,
At least for my parents, it was a choice,
But circumstances always make it seem that way,

Before we fly out, my grandmother passes away,
As I look at her wrapped in white, I think about for her, it wasn't really a choice,

When her father died, came the first split,
Her brother stayed with her mother,
As she was shuttled away to her grandparents,
Jostled into sweetness, they enjoyed the spoils of their sugar plantation,
But envy rots the fruit,
And nothing quite unleashes *nazar* as opportunity,
The partition justified revenge and jealousy,
When my great-great grandparents chose to stay in their homeland,
It wasn't to be the case,

It was 10pm,
The butler rushes in,
Despite being Hindu, he shouted the warning,
The locals were coming,
By midnight they would be here,
It will all be burned to the ground,
The sugar will melt,
And so would they all,

At only 3, my grandmother didn't quite understand,
But seeing her family rush to carry jewels and gold in their hands,
She grabbed her sandals to do what she can,
Before the fire could make it to their estate,
Off they went on their escape,
A life in Pakistan soon they would have to make,

When sugar burns,
It can burn into caramel.

2k

transpose me to the top of K2,
cut me up, segment me,
until i am fully reflected on the fallen snow,
haul the pieces i don't know how to sew back together,
in an off-brand jeep up the cliffside,
just make sure to honk loudly,
to scare away the mountain goats,

dice me finely, but do it poorly,
use a dull knife from a box set,
picked up without curation,
from the discount section at walmart,

in my current form,
i don't know,
how to make it up there,
without making friends with avalanches,
and stumbling down to the depths below,

in false memories,
it looks at me a stern grandfather,
disappointed at my inability,
to stake ice spears in his flesh,
and anchor myself to our history,

unspool me,
until i am a rope so frayed,
that the biggest needle can't thread,

all of these strings,
where do they go?

snakes writhing out of a worn basket,
i've given up on any chance of charming them back in,

perhaps the peak,
my body cannot know,
but i'm desperate, if you can find me a brush stroke on the
landscape painting,
it could be just a hill,
on the precipice of the definition of a mountain,
just enough to join the range,

if you could consider me family,
grandfather please, just a spot in the Karakoram is enough for
me.

asterisk

I have seen the banyan trees,
While walking through the rural towns of Indonesia,
But it doesn't count —

I have seen the mangroves,
While cascading down a river boat in Trinidad,
But it doesn't count —

I have tasted the sweet mangoes,
In a Mexican superstore,
But it doesn't count —

I have felt the sweltering heat,
Riding a camel in the Sahara Desert,
But it doesn't count —

All these ersatz experiences,
Just alternates,
I should have known these memories,
In my homeland,
If only if only if I grew up in my birthplace,

Instead, my feet have traversed the world,
Living in limbo as a third-world girl,

I have no claim left,
I sold my citizenship for the new world,

I can only come here as a visitor,
A stamp, a visa, a NICOP,
Traded in my green passport for the access of the blue,

These are not your senses,
This is not your banyan trees,
This is not your mangroves,
This is not your mangoes,
This is not your heat,

Always an asterisk,
I've been everywhere,
But it doesn't count.

KHI

out the gate,
and when the humidity of an unconditioned atrium wraps
around me,
i am not sure whether it comes,
with a warm hug for a long-gone family member,
a sun kissed greeting,
or whether it's sizing me up,
asking with steel on its tongue,
can you cut it?

we all make this pilgrimage,
in the winters where the continent's heat does not rake coals over
our now paled skin,

all high and mighty,
glitz and glamor,
looking down at the locals who never left,

so why can't we stand in a damn line,
with decency?
a Kafkaesque snake, with intruders slicing their own place in,
even I glimpse more than once at the *unaccompanied women and
children only* queue,
much shorter, but at the cost of my western feminist sensibilities,

out the airport,
and i tell myself it's the jetlag,
not an uncertain heat,
that pulls me out of consciousness.

parro pappo

A letter to my aunt,
Who made herself small,
To make everyone else big,

A letter to my aunt,
Who let illness take her life,
Rather than let others know she's sick,

A letter to my aunt,
How I imagine a different path for you,
Wish you could run wild down the streets,
Let your hair catch the wind and be free,

Shrunk down to nothing,
A voice that becomes a whisper,

A letter to my aunt,
A mother to no one,
Who became a mother to us all,
We remember you in every hug,
In every loving kiss,

But to put your life on hold,
No one asked for this,
A gift not worth giving,
If this is the price you paid,

This letter to you I should have long ago gave,
If you were still here,
How I wish someone gave you permission to live life your own way.

background

If you zoomed out,
Of the beautiful family photo,
You will see us, erased in the background,
The invisiblized labor that day in night out,
Manages the minutiae of your daily lives,

We might not be educated,
But it is I, the *massi*, who wakes your child for school and presses his uniform, and walks him through his evening homework,

I might not have a home of my own,
But it is I who knows every inch of your kitchen, as you call my name a million times

— More chai for the guests!
— Where are my morning paratha and eggs?
— Can you boil the water? I slept all day and want a warm bath.

And when you wake up in the afternoon to head out for another 'outing,' don't forget us, your drivers,

I might not be able to read or write,
But without me, how will you navigate the chaotic streets of this city?

While you get your hair done at the salon for hours,
Who else is watching the car in the melting heat?

Always someone else to clean, always someone else to open the door,
All your wealth atrophying independence,
And how much of your child did you even raise?

The unsung underbelly, without which you'd fall apart,
If you turn on the light,
You'll see us in the shadows.

an ancient memory

excited, my mother and her siblings arrive at their childhood home,
in the car, they reminisce,
about the beautiful trees sunlight shone through,
of their neighbors walking over for a cup of chai,
in the backseat, i await with anticipation as well,

but the broken road, with its cracks and gaps,
was an omen of what's to come,
miles of drive were akin to decades,

their faces fall,
as they see the trash littering the abandoned gardens,
the decaying gate and the worn fence,
desolate, without children playing or the scent of afternoon tea,
their eyes dart around, trying to find a hint of a beauty that has long faded,

my mother murmurs to herself,
what happened to this place?

a decaying city,
pushing down hopes of a better future,
the fate of karachi so uncertain,

how do we dig it back up?
how do we improve?
tethered to only memories,
a narrative that trails...

1254

An aged red swing,
Scratched plastic barely hanging on a thread,
Dangling limply from the ceiling,
Like an elderly spider running out of web,

My most vivid memories of my nana's home,
Was swinging, spiraling, dizzy,
A woozy ruckus of laughter,
As my cousins spun me faster and faster,

I was 10 when I last seen the rouge relic,
It's been 18 years, and nothing remains,
Not the swing,
Not the house,
A scattering, as we all moved to our own places,

If only I could swing back,
And see my aunts and uncles as kids,
Doing the same as we did,
While my grandfather warns to get down, it's not safe,

If only I could walk through the roofless veranda and once again feel the rain pour down, as we splash in the puddles of a monsoon summer,

If only the tiny tv still bustled with static,
So, I could challenge my relatives for control of the remote,

If only the sole good pillow remained,
So, I could snatch it first and go to bed before anyone else did,

Instead, I am now shuttled in a rickshaw,
From the outskirts of the city to the bustling center, to the foreign lands of suburbia,

At 1254 Federal District B you will not find my nana's home,
You'll find a new development,
Constructed by someone else, for someone else,

Will they put in a new swing?
One with well-fastened chains?
Will the parents watch,
Will the kids play?

Who's going to take care of nana?

And after all the work you do,
Putting others before you,
What is there to do?

Clearly something is broken,
When our elders are tossed aside,
Without the safety net promised,
By a culture that traded your life for your children's,
All these sacrifices made,
The trouble and toil worn as wrinkles on your face,

When your family doesn't call,
When your sons and daughters -in law rule supreme,
When your sons and daughters let you rot and fester,
And all in all, your family finally falls,

Hatred that shows passive aggressive,
When they hide your pills or deny you food,
The betrayal brazen,
When your children become your warden,
Shunned to a cage,
Nowhere to go and who's to blame?

Hatred that festers over years of disconnect,
Eventually they show their disrespect,
At your weakest and most vulnerable,
You learn all the mistakes,
Of painting your children with your own brushstrokes, you never got to place,

A cycle that doesn't break until we break it,
When your life is yours to make it,
Take me to the future, where children are nurtured and elders are cherished,

It's a hidden darkness,
Easy to ignore when age sets in,
The abuse that weaves into generations,
Revenge served with nothing else,
Vindication can only come with resolution,

We will age,
Who will be there willingly when we do?

Photographing Karachi

as a photographer,
you have a responsibility,
to be thoughtful to your subject,

to give dignity,
even in spaces where you're slammed in the face,
with the indignity, the injustice of it all,

i try my best —
if i angle my camera just right,
maybe you won't see the trash so abundant,
that every step is a tripping hazard,

maybe you don't notice,
the begging children glued to stalling cars,

at least through this picture,
you can't pick up the acrid nasal-curing,
burning gutters,

trek over to the affluent neighborhoods,
just to take a break from the contortions,
as i crop out all the ugly,

if you squint just right,
you can ignore all the problems,
the beauty of longstanding buildings,
a palm tree framed against the sky,
not the homeless underneath,
sheltering under faded cardboard,

maybe this overpriced lens,
can see something worthwhile,
through layers of dust,
through layers of protection,

there's enough poverty porn out there already,
how can there be hope for something better,

if the only representation of yourself is of all the shadows

no highlights?

basharam

another day, another dirty look,
as i fail again to meet my mother's expectations,

a dirty look,
like i am a feral child,
to be scrubbed clean,
before presenting to society,

in those moments,
i know she wishes she could drag me to the bathtub,
like when i was young,
and scrub me down raw,
insisting i would be clean,
when all the dirt was scraped out and drained away,

basharam, she calls me,
as i fail again to stay on the balance beam,
of polite propriety,

in those moments,
i know she wishes she could pull out the scissors,
and cut out all the mistakes i keep making,
as if they were clothes that didn't make the cut of modesty,
as if the single slice,
could shred away all her pain.

another dirty look,
but this time i wonder,
if it doesn't contain a bit more than disgust,
judgement laced with envy,

layers of jealousy,
of a life denied to her,

when the walls are embedded with electric shock,
it's impossible to imagine,
out of the box,

i cannot help but wonder,
if underneath the layers,
of daughter wife and mother,
she, as herself, would have wanted,
the same things as me,
but was denied everything,
and offered only purity.

To all the women who had sacrificed

To all the women who had sacrificed,
Let me be ardently clear,
That none of it was fair,
Even when it was needed,
It was too much of a burden to bear,

To all the who had sacrificed,
Their hopes and their dreams,
Sacrifices buried under the mantra of
This is how it is supposed to be,

One day every girl realizes,
The punishment of her gender,
When a trait that felt as benign as your hair color,
Begins to define the boundaries of the world you're allowed to discover,
Begins to set electric fences and a tunnel that narrows,

To all the women who had sacrificed,
Know that it was all political,
When the line was set, and set you apart,
From your brothers and your father,
From the boys who were allowed to stay out late,
While the responsibility of family was yours to face,

A body that has served you well,
That let you run down the playground,
Or climb up the hill,
Now becomes an object beyond your control,

The south asian gaze will make hypocritical demands,
Be desirable but modest,
Care about your appearance, but don't be vain,
Be likeable, but don't draw attention,
Be beautiful, but never know you're beautiful,

How many hours have we sacrificed cutting ourselves up,
A collage to fit a broken image?
It is done so insidiously that,
Sacrifice itself becomes the honor,

The pain we wear as a badge,
And turn our ire to the women who won't sacrifice the same way,
Who won't put their hopes and dreams on the shelf,
Who won't sit by — to rust, to dust,

To the women who had sacrificed,
I feel your anger,
That some have escaped the prison you've made your own,
And it's funny that maybe you wouldn't have minded the pain,
If the choice was truly your own,

Labor that takes a cost,
But never offers a wage,
Wrapped up in childbirth, it seems we were made for pain,
To carry baskets around for others to fill,
Never minding the holes, or the overflowing water that already spills,

And if your children aren't grateful,
And your husband never cares,
What was the point of such sacrifice,
If it turned your sweet soul so bitter?

The walls that close in,
Eventually your spirit is squashed,

To all the women who sacrificed,
I ask you to grieve,
Because at some point, you were a girl like me,
With hopes and dreams,
This cruel world took away,
But if you're alive, please know,
This, we're trying to change,

So the responsibility doesn't lay on the shoulders of our sisters,
It's easy to say from this platform, this place,
But i promise you, this change will extend to each woman,
All those unnoticed, and forgotten,
It's a change that cannot rest,
Until it reaches every garment worker toiling in Bangladesh,
Until it cripples to our rejoice, not our pain,

To every woman who has sacrificed,
You still have time to gain,
Back your hopes and your dreams,
It may not feel yet like so,
Perhaps your dreams at twenty,
Will come true at seventy,

You will find yourself and let go,
Of that broken image of a perfect dutiful woman,
And cut beyond those electric fences,
And push the walls out, with the strength beyond childbirth,
And live in a world that expands,

You are more than a daughter, sister, wife, or mother.

Perhaps you cannot believe me yet,
It takes too much to trust, our fragile hearts cannot bear,
The pain is fine but hope,
It's hope that is devastating,

Forgive me for all the times I did not understand,
I'll forgive you for all the times you judged,

To the women who sacrificed for me,
May your sacrifice be needed no more,
Without your healing, we are going nowhere,
To be happy is sometimes the harder burden to bear.

what it means to be a woman

i have always admired the elegance of the sari,
the iconic Bollywood fashion statement,
hair pinned, eyes painted with *kajil*, and wrapped under layers of femininity and mystique,
in my tomboyish t shirt and jeans it seems so distant,
try as i might, i can't pin the *pallu* just right,
i do my best, and my mother says,
well, that's not how you wear it,
so many options,
nivi, open, bengali, gol, dhoti,

all the ways to be a woman,
who are we to say?
how the fabric wraps? where the pin's placed?

What your mother tells you

I am trying to reconcile,
The pain of a child,
And the wisdom of an adult,

When I am hurting,
She tells me she loves me and asks for a hug,
But I lash out instead and cast her aside,
I know I should ask for her forgiveness,
But I am also trying to forgive her,

We give our children what we want,
At the expense of what they need,
Add in an immigration story,
And distance forms the recipe,

I wanted to call this poem
The things my mother told me
And lay out her mistakes like a sentence,
One count of neglect,
One count of judgment,
One count of internalized sexism,
One count of just not getting it,

But that feels cruel, I see her crestfallen face,
When I point out all the ways her soul has bruised mine,

How could I admonish her for not being the archetype mother, who lavishes support and nurture,
When my nana never even told her she loved her?
How could I expect hours of attention, when coming to America already stole her vitality and patience?
Let's not even get into explaining the foreign concept of a care package!

I want to say my mother never taught me the secrets of girlhood,
But how could I? When she comes to me now, insecure, asking how to put on makeup?

How can I point out all the rules she placed, when the burden of culture is a mother's weight?
If I cross a line, we all know which parent is to blame,
How could I compare her to sitcom moms who have it all?
When our society sets women up to fail and to fall?

When I separate my mother from motherhood, I feel her pain,
Of all the sacrifices made only to have it thrown back into your face,
I'm being cruel I know, I need to learn to let go,
The standards that aren't fair, of a fantasy impossible for any woman to achieve,

I am trying to let her in, to feel close to me now,
To meet in a halfway place between our worlds,

The things my mother told me,
Are melting away,
As I am full of the things, to my mother, I want to say,

That it wasn't enough, but that's okay,
It's a burden we'll share, let's move beyond blame,
Your sacrifices have given me the space for healing,
To know better and to do better,
Are luxuries denied to you, but abundant to me,

It's a fragile space we are in,
I breathe slowly,
It's so tender,
I'm trying to keep it afloat.

Legacy

a growth in the womb,
anxieties flurry over me,
in the shadows
a cancer waiting to metastasize,
if i fail to consider fully,
all the things,
we threaten to pass down,

born with cracks,
not everyone knows how to heal,
this generational trauma,
unchecked — spreads,
until even the most resilient souls crack,

i worry if an unretrievable outburst,
will pour out of me,
that i too,
will point out every flaw,
every social deformity,
that doesn't fit the rigid mold,
i was told to be,

will i do enough,
to sway away from such pain?
does my grandmother know the damage she'd verberate?
echoes of history,
we must radicalize instead,
towards passionate change,

may my daughters,
and my daughters' daughters,
never have the cloud of conditional love,
cross their starry nights,

may my sons,
and my sons' sons,
never wonder if something is wrong with them,
if they dare to cry,

a growth in the womb,
what do we choose to remove?
perform this surgery,
and cut out these festering wounds,

it can't serve me to stay the same,
soothe into a new world,
diamonds don't need such pressure to form,
my sons and daughters,
it's love and only love we will forge.

Native (ii.)

The years have passed,
The aches of ancestral pain have faded,
Leaving something close to peace,

When you run,
Don't forget what runs in the family,
What traits have woven into your thread,
What's the story you want to create,

Now sights are set to the horizon,
The only way forward is to set off to sea,
To rebuild Noah's ark and take it with you,
What we want to keep, what we leave to rust on the dock,
Tumors cut out,
A clamoring as it all hits the ground,
Anchors casted off,
It's all burdens lifted,

Sew your sails with lightness,
Decorate the mast with what life means to you,
A family that becomes a crew,
Ropes gathering, direction steering,
All in harmony, all synchronizing,
But only when you put in the work,
Only when you shine light into all of the dark,

Let the salty wind smooth over all the bruises,
Let the waves guide your meditation,
Pull out your spyglass and find adventure,
Draw out the map as you discover,
All the new ways to be,

All my relatives shine,
The sky is full of our constellation,
You can find our names in the stars,
Our family history is complete,
Even in the night, the ocean is bright with our bioluminescence,

Righteous compass, your soul will know,
Close your eyes, climb aboard,
The future awaits.

About the Author

Vareesha Khan is a multi-media storyteller working as an art director in advertising. Karachi-born, she moved at a young age to the United States and Canada. She blends a variety of media to create meaningful experiences, rallying people around the idea that human connection is the foundation for a better world. In addition to her written work, she performs poetry in Chicago and pursues photography and fine arts in her free time.

www.ingramcontent.com/pod-product-compliance
Lightning Source LLC
Chambersburg PA
CBHW042350040426
42449CB00018B/3476